Fairy Tales

THE STORY OF THE UGLY DUCKLING

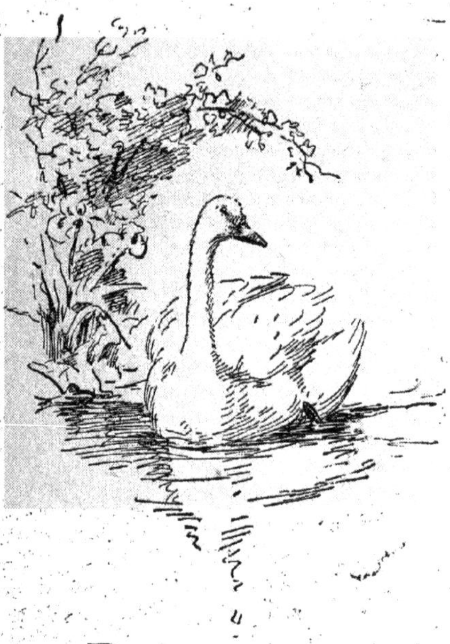

Aunt Ella

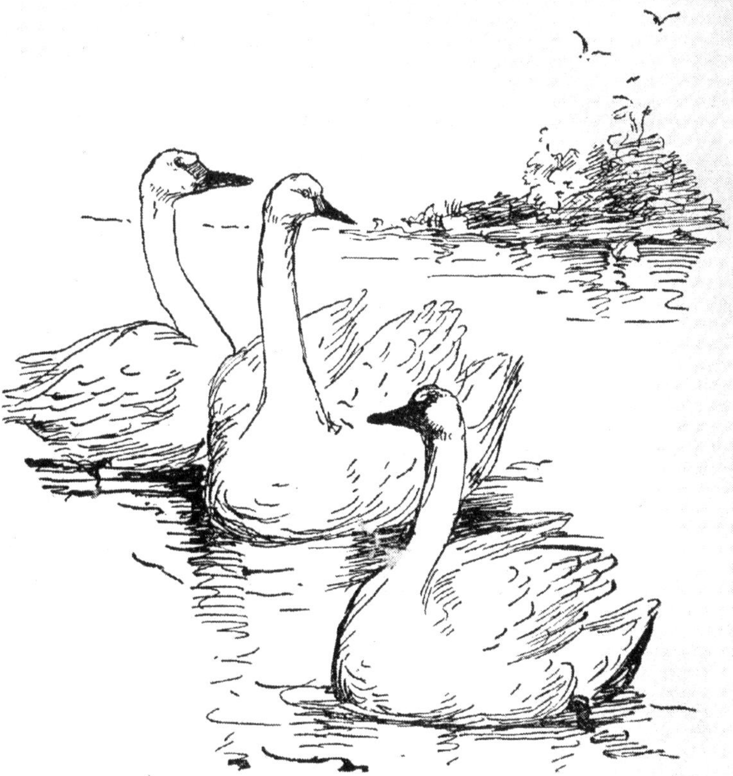

One day as the sun was setting there came a great flock of splendid birds out of the bushes. They were pure white with long necks; they were swans.

THE
UGLY DUCKLING

In the lovely country it was summer-time. The cornfields were ripe. The oats were green. The hay stood in its tall stacks, and the storks walked about on their long red legs.

Yes, it was a fair, fair country. In the midst of all this beauty and sunshine there stood an old farm with deep canals around it. Near the water was a high wall with bushes growing tall; it was like a deep wood among those bushes and there, upon her nest, sat a duck to hatch her young ones.

Day after day she kept at her task and ere the little ones came she was very tired. She was lonely too

for no one came to see her. The other ducks would rather swim on the canals than talk to her.

But at last one of the eggs cracked. How eagerly the duck now watched her nest! Another and another egg did the same.

"Peep! Peep!" cried each little duck as it put forth a soft, downy, yellow head. And "What a big, big world!" they all exclaimed, for surely the nest was larger than the egg shell.

"Do you think that this is all the world?" asked the proud mother. "Why, this is not much! The world runs way up there across the garden. I have never been so far, but it is quite true for all that."

"Now are you all here?" she asked as she carefully looked about. "No. That large egg is still not hatched. How long is that to last, I wonder?"

But she sat down again.

"How goes it?" asked an old Duck who had heard the news about the new family and had waddled down to see for herself.

"This one egg lasts a very long time," replied the patient mother. "It will not burst. But just look at the little ducks! Are they not sweet? They all look exactly like their father, the dears! But he, the bad fellow, does not come to see me."

"Let me see the egg that will not burst," said the old Duck. "Ah, it is a turkey egg! I was once fooled that way. I had great trouble, for turkeys are afraid of the water. They will never venture on it. You had better leave that egg and go and teach your other children how to swim."

"I'll stay a little longer," answered the mother. "I have sat so long that a few more days now will not matter."

"Just as you please," said the old Duck coldly as she walked off.

At last the egg burst.

"Peep! Peep!" said the little one, and out it crept from the shell.

It was very ugly.

"It is not like the others!" wailed the mother. "Can it be a turkey chick? We will soon find out. It shall go into the water if I have to push it in!"

The next day was bright and fair. The mother duck went early to the pond with all her little ones, and it was indeed a pretty sight.

"Splash!" into the water she went.

"Quack! Quack!" she called. That meant "Come! Come!" as every one of the little ducks knew and in they followed one after the other. The water closed over them—but what did they care? Their legs went as easily as could be. It was great sport!

And the ugly little duck was there too, swimming with the rest.

"It is not a turkey chick!" exulted the mother duck. "It is my very own child. And if you look at it the right way it is not very ugly. Come, my dears, I will take you to the barnyard and show you the

great world. Now keep close to me. Some one might tread on you. And look out for cats!"

There was a hot battle going on in the barnyard. Two parties were fighting desperately for a fish's head, and in the end the cat got it all.

"That's the way of the world!" cried the mother duck, and she sharpened her beak. Ah! how she wanted the fish head!

"Use your legs!" she commanded her family. "Hurry about and bow your heads to the old Duck over there. She's the grandest of them all. She has  Spanish blood in her, and that is why she is so fat. And do you see that she has a red rag around her leg? That is something fine—the greatest thing a duck can have. It means that her owner does not want to lose her. Don't turn in your toes! A well-bred duck always turns them out like father and mother. Now bend your necks and say 'Rap!'"

And they did so; but the other ducks cried coldly:

"Were there not enough ducks here without all these? And look at that ugly one over there! We won't stand that!" and one flew up and bit the poor little gray thing in the neck!

"Oh, shame!" cried out the mother duck. "She is doing no harm!"

"But she's too large and queer," cried the duck who had bitten it, "and so we will tease her!"

Just then the old duck with the rag on her leg said slowly: "Those are pretty children that the mother has there, all but one; that one is a failure. I wish she could make it pretty like the rest."

"That I cannot do, my lady," said the poor mother. "She is not pretty but she is very sweet, and she swims just as well as the others. She may grow pretty," and she smoothed its feathers.

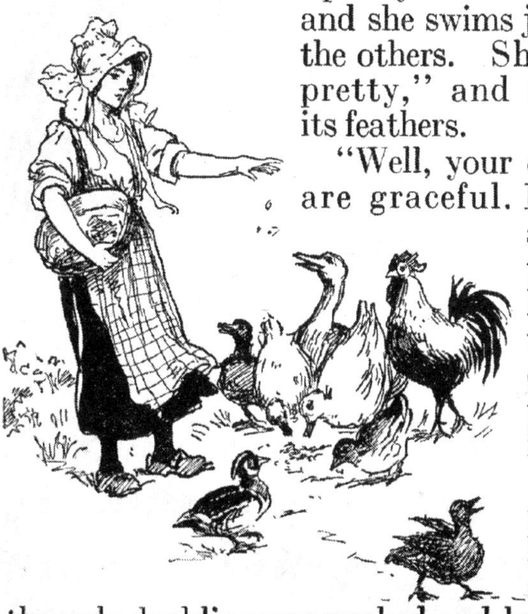

"Well, your other children are graceful. Make yourself at home and the next fish head you see, take it. But do not eat it—you may bring it to me!"

Soon after they went home, and all along the way the ugly duckling was pushed and hurt and jeered.

That was the first day. And as time went on things steadily grew worse and worse.

Her own brothers and sisters were cruel to her and at every turn she was made to suffer. Even her mother wished that the ugly child was far away. As she grew big she flew over the fence, and the little birds were afraid of her. If she went into the barnyard the girl who fed the fowls kicked her with her foot.

"It is because I am so very ugly," cried the poor little thing in despair, and one day she flew away to the wild ducks who lived out on the wide moor. Here she lay sad and tired.

When the wild ducks saw her, they said, "What sort of a duck are you?"

And then when the poor thing tried to make a bow as best she could, they only jeered at her effort to be polite.

"You are very ugly," they laughed, "but we do not mind if you do not marry into our family."

Marry! Poor little duckling, she had not thought of such a thing. She only wanted to find a home where she could rest and have a quiet drink from the river.

So she stayed two days. Then a pair of very saucy ganders came by. They were young and wanted to have a good time.

"You are so ugly that we like you," said they.

"Will you come with us and be a bird that flies from place to place? Near here there are some lovely wild geese. We are quite sure that one of them would say 'Rap!' to you if you asked one to marry you."

"Piff! Paff!" a shot rang out. One of the young ganders fell dead.

"Paff! Piff!" spoke another gun. And the second saucy young gander fell as the first.

A great hunt was going on. The water was red with blood. The ugly duckling had never been so frightened. She put her head under her wing, and when she had gathered enough courage to look out again, what do you think she saw?

A frightful great dog, with his tongue hanging far out!

He tried to snap at her, but she knew the land was no place for her. Into the water she went, and the dog ran on.

"I am so ugly," cried she, "that even the dog runs away!"

So she lay still at the water's edge, hidden by some overhanging bushes. She listened intently as the shots grew further and further apart. Finally they ceased altogether.

When she had assured herself that the hunt was really over, she climbed up the bank and walked sadly on. The sun sank lower and lower in the west. Another day was almost done. When it had dipped below the horizon and even the last of its beautiful afterglow had faded and night was indeed near the ugly duckling came to a poor hut. She saw that the one door stood partly open. With the night there had come a storm and as the wind was blowing wildly, the duckling crept into the hovel to find both shelter and rest.

Now in this poor hut there lived a woman with her cat and her hen. The cat she called Sonnie! He could arch his back, and he could purr, and he could make sparks fly from his eyes.

The hen had short legs but a long name. The woman called her Chick-a-biddy-short-shanks. And as she laid good eggs and many of them, the woman loved her as her own child.

Now when the cat and the hen saw the poor duckling the cat purred and the hen clucked.

The old woman could not see very well, and for a time she did not see the duck. When she did she was glad for, as she had no duck of her own, she thought it was quite a prize.

But the hen and the cat did not like to have anyone share their home, selfish creatures that they were, and were so cross that the duckling sat lonely enough in her corner.

One day she longed so to have a swim that she told the hen all about it.

"What a queer thought!" scoffed the hen. "If you had more to do you would not have time to be thinking of such silly things."

"But it is lovely to swim on the water," insisted the duckling. "It is fine to dive down to the bottom."

"You must be crazy," replied the hen. "I am sure you are crazy. At any rate, you had better ask the cat about it. He is the wisest creature I know roundabout here. Ask him if he likes to swim on the water. Ask the old woman. I do not think they would care to go diving down to the bottom of the water."

"You don't know what I mean!" cried the duckling in despair.

"No, we do not," answered the hen. "But who does, pray? You had better be thankful you have enough food and a warm home, and stop talking so silly."

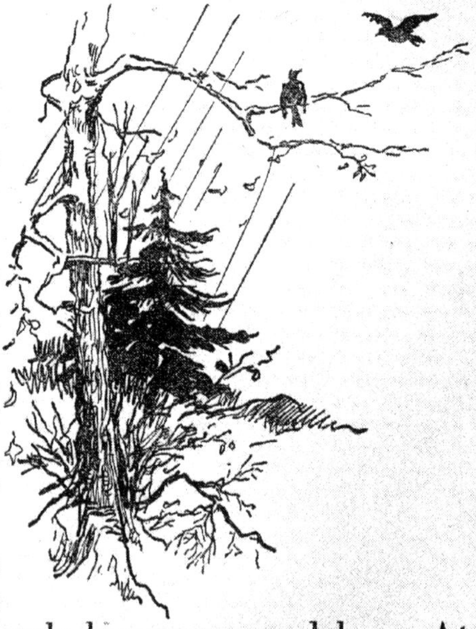

"I think I will go away," at last the duckling thought, "away into the great wide world."

And she went. She soon found the water and swam and dived. Oh, it was good! But it was the same story —every bird and beast hurt her, or was afraid of her.

Then came the autumn. The leaves fell. The clouds hung gray and low. At last the snowflakes whirled through the chill air.

One day as the sun was setting there came a great flock of splendid birds out of the bushes. They were pure white with long necks; they were swans.

They gave a long, low cry, spread out their beautiful strong wings and flew away to warmer lands.

So high, so high they went! And the ugly duckling felt very queer as she watched them go. She turned round and round in the water, and then she too gave a long, low cry. It almost made her afraid, that cry she uttered.

She could not forget the lovely white birds, and

she knew that soon she would see them no more.

She dived to the bottom of the river, and when she came up she was almost beside herself with grief. She knew not the name of the wonderful birds, nor where they had gone, but she did know that she loved them every one.

She did not envy them. She could not be like them. But oh! she loved them. Poor little ugly duckling!

The winter grew cold! The duckling had to swim around a great deal to keep the water from freezing in the river. But in spite of all her efforts each night the hole in which she swam grew smaller and smaller and smaller. She  had to keep her legs going all the time until at last, quite worn out with her efforts, she sat still and the water froze about her. But early in the morning a man passing by saw the poor duckling and he broke the ice and carried her to his home. The children wanted to play with her but that made her afraid and she flew into the milk pan and the flour. At which the mother struck at her with a stick and that made her still more afraid. But just then the door was flung open. The poor duckling flew out and dropped half dead upon the snow.

I will not try to tell you how dreadful that long, cold winter was to the poor duckling. It would make your hearts far too sad to hear.

Then spring came. The sun shone warm, the larks sang as they pierced the sky, and the duckling could flap her weak wings.

Each day her wings grew stronger and soon, without knowing just how it happened, she found herself in a lovely garden where bright flowers blossomed and shed their perfume on the warm air, and a canal ran near by.

This was fine indeed! And then one day there came three dear white swans and they swam on the canal.

The duckling knew them. Had she not thought of them every day the long winter through?

She said sadly, "I will fly to them and tell them how I suffer. They may kill me because I am so very ugly, but I do not care. I would far rather die than be beaten and left to live another winter."

The duckling flew out on the canal and the three swans saw it and came with spread wings.

"Kill me!" cried the poor duckling as she bent her head.

What did she see? She saw herself in the water, and lo! no longer was she a gray ugly duckling, hateful to look upon—she was a swan!

It did not matter if she were born in a duck yard; she had come out of a swan egg.

The swans came nearer, and touched her with their beaks. Into the garden came some little children and they threw bread to the swans. The youngest child cried, "There is a new swan!" and all  the rest shouted, "Yes, a new one, and it is the sweetest of all! So young! So pretty!"

She was so happy she did not know what to do; all the old trouble was gone and from her glad heart she cried, "I never dreamed of so much joy when I was an ugly duckling!"

THE
TIN
SOLDIER

There were twenty-five tin soldiers once on a time. They were all brothers, for they had all been made out of one old spoon. They had muskets, and they all looked right in front of them. Their clothes were red and blue, and I tell you they were a fine lot.

The first words they ever heard as the lid was taken off their box were "Tin Soldiers!" A little boy had spoken the words, and he clapped his hands in joy.

It was his birthday, and when he had looked at them he put them on the table.

All the Tin Soldiers were alike but one. There had not been enough tin to finish him so he had only one leg. But he stood on that as well as the others did on two legs, and this soldier was to be greater than all the other twenty-four.

On the table were many toys besides the soldiers, and the best was a paper castle.

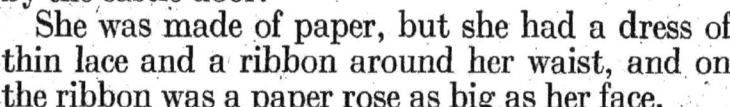

If one looked in the windows one could see the hall, and in front of it were some trees and a lake made of a bit of glass.

Wax swans swam on the lake; it was all very pretty, but the sweetest of all was a small lady who stood by the castle door.

She was made of paper, but she had a dress of thin lace and a ribbon around her waist, and on the ribbon was a paper rose as big as her face.

The little lady held her arms up for she was a dancer, and she held one leg so high that the Tin Soldier could not see it at all, and he thought that she had but one leg.

"She would be just the wife for me," he thought, "but she is too grand. She lives in a castle, and I have only a box, and so many of us live in the box! It really is no place for her."

But he felt he must know her. He lay down behind a box and watched her all day. There she stood on one leg; she did not seem to get tired at all.

At night the toys began to have their fun. They played war; they gave balls and paid visits.

The Nut Cracker jumped up and down. The Pencil ran about on a piece of paper, and they all made so much noise that the bird in its cage woke up and began to talk. The only ones who could not join the fun were the Tin Soldiers and the Dancing Lady. (You know the soldier with one leg was not in the box with his brothers, but was hid behind another box.)

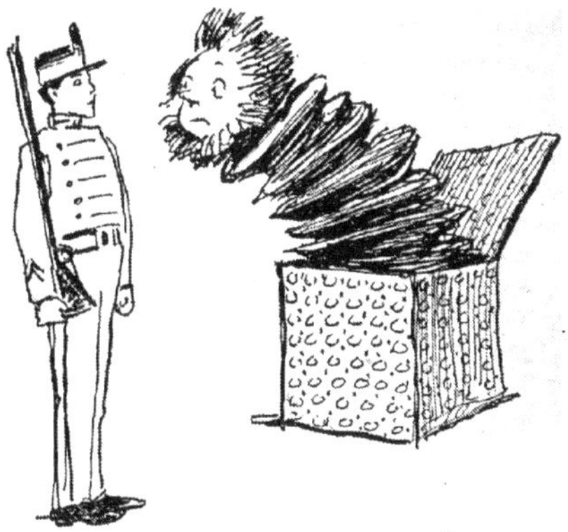

The clock struck twelve—and bounce! The lid flew off the box behind which was the Soldier, and as true as I tell you out of the box came a Goblin. You see it was a trick!

"Tin Soldier," said the Goblin, "do not stare so at what does not concern you."

The Soldier did not seem to hear.

"Just you wait until tomorrow!" said the Goblin.

The next day when the children came the Tin Soldier was put in the window, and I do not know whether it was the Goblin or the wind who caught him, but heels over head the poor Soldier fell from the third story to the street.

The nurse and the little boy came down at once to look for him. If he had only cried out, "Here I am!" they would have heard him, but he was too brave to cry.

Then it began to rain and soon the streets were full of water. Two boys came by and one cried, "Oh, look! There's a Tin Soldier!" And they made a paper boat and sailed him down the gutter.

Oh, dear! how high the waves were in that gutter! Still the Tin Soldier stood firm and looked right in front of him, just like a true Soldier does in danger.

All at once the boat went into a dark place.

"Where am I going now?" thought he. "This is the Goblin's fault. Ah! if the little lady was in the boat with me I would not mind the dark."

But just then a Water Rat jumped out in front of the boat. "Give me your passport!" said he. The Soldier held his gun close and said not a word.

But the stream grew stronger. The Tin Soldier could see the light beyond and he heard a great noise that would have made even you afraid. Only think right ahead was a deep river, and for that little Soldier in his tiny boat that was an awful thing. The boat sailed on and the Soldier stood stiff and not even an eye winked.

The boat turned around three times. The water came in. The Tin Soldier stood up to his neck in it; then it closed over his head. He thought of the sweet lady, and a song came to him as he sank:

"Farewell, farewell, thou warrior brave,
For this day thou must die!"

The boat broke in two parts, and just at that moment a great fish snapped the Tin Soldier.

Well, it was dark in the fish's body! And it was small too. The Tin Soldier could only lie straight and not turn around. The fish swam to and fro, but before long he was caught on a hook, and then light shone on the Tin Soldier and some one cried, "The Soldier!" It was strange but the cook at the little boy's house had bought the fish and when she cut it open she saw the Soldier and took him to the room above to show to the children.

It was the same dear room, and the children and toys, but best of all there was the Dancing Lady! The Soldier almost cried when he saw her, but they looked at each other and said not a word.

Then one of the boys without any reason took the poor Soldier and flung him into the fire. I am sure it was the Goblin who made him do it.

The Soldier stood still in the awful heat; the color of his coat melted away. He looked at the dear little lady and she looked at him. He felt as if he were melting but he stood firm.

Then the wind caught the Dancing Lady, and she flew through the air like a bird and came right in the fire near the Tin Soldier. A flash, and she was gone into the blaze!

The Tin Soldier melted in a lump at first and then he melted into the shape of a heart. The little lady was all gone, only the rose she had worn was left, and that was black as the coal.

THE
PRINCESS ON THE PEA

There was once a Prince who wanted to be married, but no one quite suited him. You see he wanted a *real* Princess, not just one who was a King's daughter. He wished her to be a Princess through and through, and it was just as hard to find one then as it is now.

He went all over the world, and he saw many, many a Princess, but there was something wrong about each one. At last he went home quite sad because he thought there were no more real Princesses.

One night when he and his father and mother sat in their castle a great storm came up. The wind blew, the rain fell in torrents and the old castle shook and swayed. All at once there was a loud knock on the door, and the old King went and opened it himself.   And there upon the steps stood a Princess!

The King knew her to be one at once.   She was wet and tired and looked forlorn, I can tell you. She said that she was a real Princess and so the Queen said she might come in out of the storm.

"We shall see if she is a real Princess," said the Queen.   "I have a sure way of finding out."

While the others were at supper she went to make the bed where the Princess was to sleep.

Now, first she put three little hard peas on the bed spring. She then laid twenty mattresses on and twenty feather beds on top of all.

And that was the bed for the Princess.

The next morning when they were all at break-fast the Queen said, "Well, my dear, did you sleep well last night?"

"Oh, no!" replied the Princess. "I did not sleep at all. I do not know what was in my bed, but it was something so hard that my body is all black and blue. It has hurt me very much."

Now the Queen was sure that here was a real Princess at last. If she could feel those peas through all those mattresses there could be no mistake. So the Prince married her and they had a fine wedding and were happy as could be.

The three peas were put where all the people could see them, and they may be there now if they are not lost!

THE
FIR
TREE

Far in the deep woods there once grew a pretty Fir Tree. It was a bright place. The sun shone on the tree, the breeze kissed it and near it grew other fir trees, some young, some old.

But the little Fir Tree was not happy. He did not care for wind or sun. He wanted to be tall! He thought of it all the time. When the boys and girls sat neath his shade and said, "What a dear little tree!" he was much vexed.

Year by year the Tree grew. A long shoot was sent out each year and by that you could tell how old the Tree was.

"I want to be tall!" he cried. "I want to be tall! Then the birds will nest in my branches and my crown shall look out at the great world!"

When snow came a little hare just for fun would run and jump over the Tree. That was hard to bear. Think of a hare jumping over you! The thought of that made the Tree forget the song of birds, the sun and the bright clouds.

Men came in the Fall and cut the tall trees down. The crash made the Fir Tree shake with fear. There they lay quite dead. Poor trees! Where were they to go? Far, far from the deep woods, but where?

One Spring when the birds had come back, the Tree said, "Know you where the tall trees have gone, my friends? Did you meet them?"

A big stork replied, "Yes, I saw them! As I flew here I met some ships. Those ships had great masts. Those tall masts were your friends, I think; they smelled like fir. You may be proud of them, they sailed so finely."

Then the Fir Tree said, "Oh, that I were tall so I might sail the sea! What is the sea? Tell me, what does it look like?"

"It would take too long to tell you," said the stork, and away he flew.

When Christmas drew near, a great many young trees were cut down, some not as tall as the Fir Tree. Then horses drew them from the woods.

"Where do they go?" asked the Fir Tree. "They are not as tall as I."

"We know," cried the birds. "We saw them in the town. There they grow in a warm room. No more cold or snow. Bright things are hung on them, and gay lights shine from their boughs."

"Oh, I wish that I might go too!" sighed the Fir Tree. "I long to go and see the world! If I am tall next year it may be they will take me. I must grow and grow!"

So through the cold and the heat the Tree grew.

Christmas drew near again. Some one saw the Fir Tree and cried: "See that fine tree!" and then the great ax struck on him and with a groan he fell to the ground. A sharp pain was all he felt. He forgot his joy.

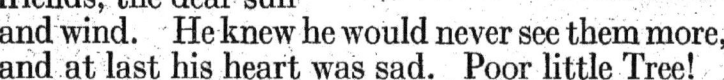

He saw his old friends, the dear sun and wind. He knew he would never see them more, and at last his heart was sad. Poor little Tree!

The next he knew, two men took him from the cold and dark into a bright room. There were toys and boys and girls, and there was a lady who hung gay things upon his branches.

"To-night," they said, "we will light the Tree."

The Fir had not thought of anything so fine. "Oh, that the trees would come from the wood to see me!" he thought. "This is life! This is joy!"

Night came. The candles were lighted. Oh, what a blaze of light! Then the doors of the room were flung back, and in came the boys and girls laughing in their delight. "Tell us a tale," cried they to a man who stood near.

Then he told them about Humpty Dumpty.

"Ah, me!" thought the Tree. "Is this true? Who knows, I too may fall down stairs, win a throne and wed a princess!"

Poor, poor Tree! You see how vain and silly he had grown. He thought about the story all night. In the dim dawn the maids came into the room.

"More joy," thought the Tree. But he was wrong. They took him with rough hands and bore him to a dark attic and there left him alone.

"It is cold!" cried the Fir Tree, "and it is so lonely here!"

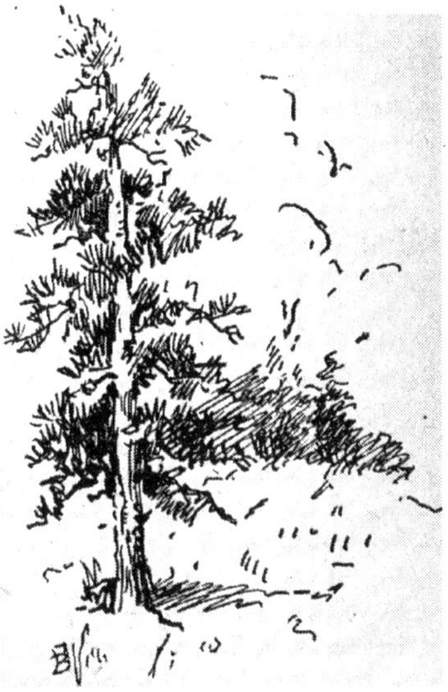

"It is cold," squeaked the mice, "but it is nice here. Tell us what you know."

"I know of the woods, where the sun shines and the wind blows." Then he told them of the night in the warm room.

"Those dear times may come again. Humpty Dumpty fell down stairs, yet won the princess."

Then the Fir Tree thought of the sweet Birch Tree in the dear old woods. What a princess she would be for him, to be sure!

One day a maid came to the attic and when she saw the Tree she took it down stairs and out into the light and air.

"Quir-ri-vir-ri-vit!" sang the birds. "My love is come!"

He knew what they meant. "I shall live!" he sang back. But no, he was thrown on a heap of weeds and boys and girls tore his branches and cried, "See the ugly old tree!"

"Oh, if I had only been content with the sun and air and birds! Too late! All is gone of my old glad life!" he thought.

All tales must end, and so the Fir Tree was burnt, and all was past.

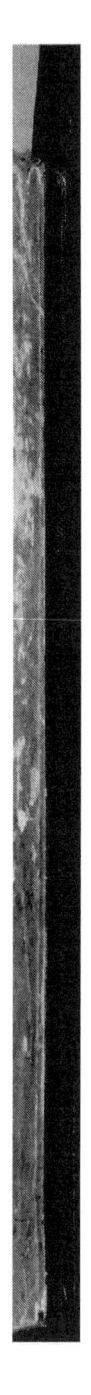

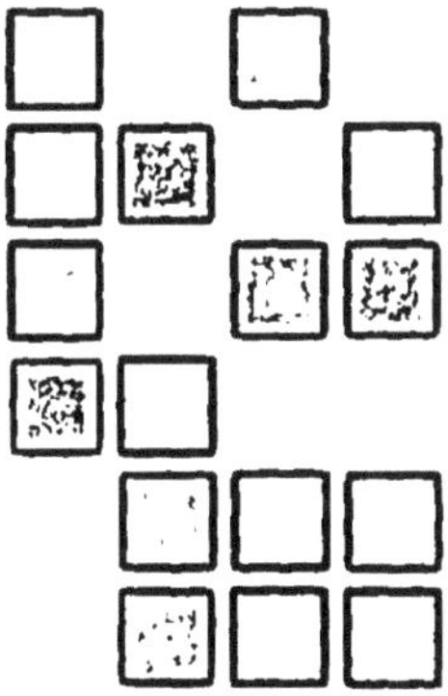

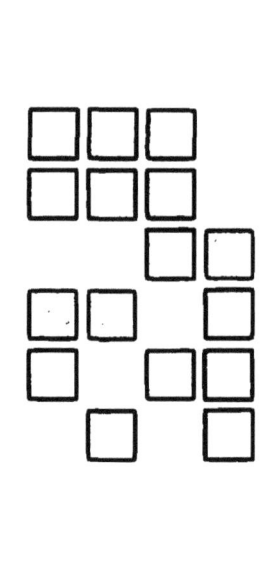

www.ingramcontent.com/pod-product-compliance
Ingram Content Group UK Ltd.
Pitfield, Milton Keynes, MK11 3LW, UK
UKHW020737210325
456550UK00005B/31